Whoopie Pies
Ooh La La!

Corinne Jausserand
photographs by Caroline Faccioli

STACKPOLE
BOOKS

0 11557 01256 9

Contents

SWEET WHOOPIE PIES

6   Classic Vanilla Whoopie Pies

8   Chocolate-Caramel Whoopie Pies

10   Cookie-Butter Whoopie Pies

12   Peanut Butter and Caramel Whoopie Pies

14   Chocolate-Hazelnut Spread Whoopie Pies

14   Triple Chocolate Whoopie Pies

16   Chestnut Cream Whoopie Pies

18   Tiramisu Whoopie Pies

20   Chocolate and Orange Whoopie Pies

22   Praline Whoopie Pies

24   Cookie Whoopie Pies

26   Banana Toffee Whoopie Pies

28   Apricot and Sesame Whoopie Pies

30   Coconut Whoopie Pies

32   Blueberry Whoopie Pies

34   Pistachio Whoopie Pies

36   Ice Cream and Pecan Whoopie Pies

38   Strawberry-Basil Whoopie Pies

40   Lavender Whoopie Pies

42   Raspberry Whoopie Pies

44   Marshmallow Whoopie Pies

46   Lemon Meringue Whoopie Pies

48   Birthday Whoopie Pie

50   Whoopie Pies à la Rose

52   Carrot Cake Whoopie Pies

SAVORY WHOOPIE PIES

54   Tomato and Tapenade Whoopie Pies

56   Feta, Thyme, and Honey Whoopie Pies

58   Parmesan Whoopie Pies with Artichoke

60   Sun-dried Tomato and Bacon Whoopie Pies

62   Buckwheat and Smoked Salmon
      Whoopie Pies

A love affair with *les whoopies*

This book, originally published in French, offers 30 recipes for delicious whoopie pies that are anything but ordinary. American visitors to Paris are often surprised to see that almost every chic bakery, or *patisserie*, in the city offers a tempting variety of whoopie pies—what the French call *les whoopies*. But these Paris treats are not the same as those found at summer picnics and farmer's markets back home.

They are whoopie pies reimagined and interpreted with a distinctly French flair—whoopie pies with chocolate and caramel, whoopie pies with lavender, whoopie pies with apricots, strawberry-basil whoopie pies, whoopie pies à la rose, even savory whoopies with feta and thyme. After all, why serve simple whoopie pies when you can serve whoopie pies ooh la la?

Making whoopie pies in 3 steps

1. **Making the cakes.** You'll need to make an even number of cakes (you'll need 2 cakes for each whoopie pie). With a pencil draw circles on a piece of parchment paper, tracing around the top of a small glass. Arrange them in staggered rows, well spaced out, since the batter will spread out and puff up while cooking. Use a pastry bag to make round, neat discs of batter inside the guide circles you drew on the parchment paper—or use a small spoon to put the batter on the pan.

    In these recipes, we make small whoopie pies, a little more than an inch in diameter. But there's no reason you can't make tiny whoopie pies as small as ¾ inch (see the lavender whoopie pies on page 40) or oversized ones as wide as 8 inches (see the birthday whoopie pie on page 48).

2. **Baking the cakes.** The baking time will depend on the size of the whoopie pies, but, in general, it's around 8 minutes. When the cakes are fully baked, remove them from the oven and let them cool to room temperature. Don't stack the cakes after removing them from the oven, as they can stick together.

3. **The filling.** The only thing left to do is to spread the filling onto the inside of a cake. The possibilities for fillings are endless—lemon cream, chocolate ganache, pistachio icing, confectioner's custard, or one of the other tasty ideas found in these pages. Put an iced cake and a plain cake together—and you have a delicious French-style *whoopie!*

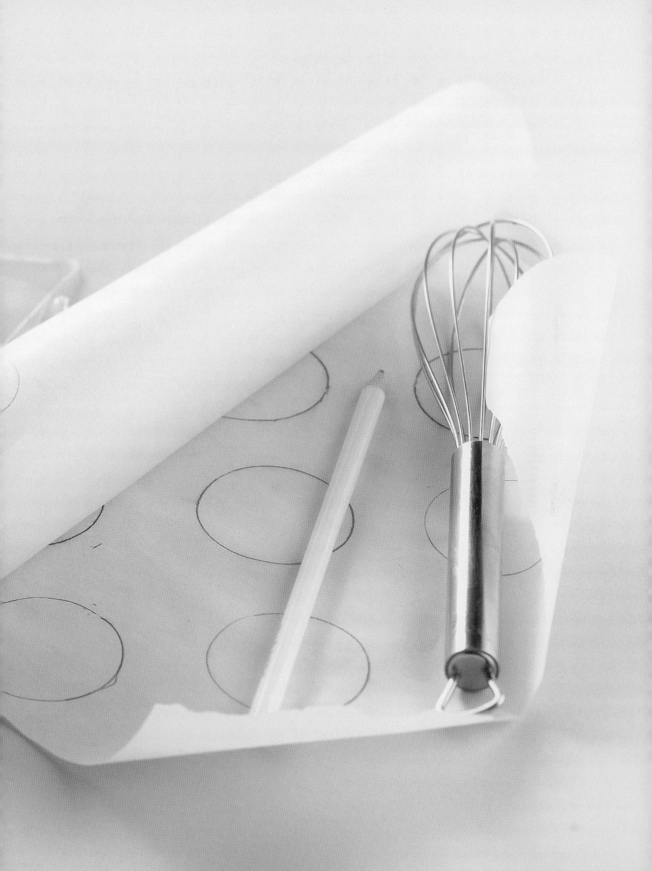

Classic vanilla whoopie pies

MAKES 20 WHOOPIE PIES ABOUT
1 IN. IN DIAMETER

PREPARATION: 25 MIN

COOKING: 8 MIN

For the cakes

⅔ c butter, softened

⅔ c sugar

3 eggs

2 c flour

1 tsp vanilla extract

1 tsp baking powder

1 tsp baking soda

For the filling

½ c light whipping cream, chilled

8 oz mascarpone*

½ c confectioner's sugar, plus
4 Tbsp for decoration

1 Tbsp vanilla extract

*Note: A few recipes in this book call for
mascarpone, a wonderful soft Italian
cheese available at specialty grocers. If
you can't find it, a good substitute for
mascarpone can be made by combining
16 oz of softened cream cheese with ¼
c of whipping cream and ½ c of sour
cream and blending until smooth.

Make the cakes. Preheat the oven to 350°. Cream the butter and
sugar until the mixture is white. Add the eggs one at a time,
beating the mixture after each egg is added. Sift in the flour and
add the vanilla, baking powder, and baking soda. Beat with an
electric mixer on medium speed for 1 to 2 minutes. The batter
should be smooth and all the ingredients should be mixed in
completely. Place the batter in small, neat circles on parchment
paper on a baking sheet (see the tips on page 4). Bake for 8
minutes. When the cakes are done, take them out of the oven
and let them cool.

Prepare the vanilla cream. Whip the cream with an electric
mixer. In a separate bowl, beat the mascarpone, ½ c of the
confectioner's sugar, and the vanilla extract. Add the whipped
cream to this mixture and mix well until it's smooth and creamy.

Fill the whoopie pies. Use a pastry bag or small spoon to spread
the vanilla cream on the flat sides of half of the cakes, then place
a plain cake on top of each iced cake, with the rounded sides
out. Dust the whoopie pies with the reserved confectioner's sugar
before serving.

Give in to the temptation of caramel-flavored chocolate. If you can't find it in the supermarket, you can easily make your own: Just add 5 Tbsp of salted butter caramel to 5 oz of melted baking chocolate.

Chocolate-caramel whoopie pies

MAKES 15 WHOOPIE PIES ABOUT
1 IN. IN DIAMETER

PREPARATION: 35 MIN

COOKING: 10 MIN

For the cakes
2 oz dark or bittersweet baking chocolate (at least 67% cacao)
⅓ c butter, softened
½ c sugar
2 eggs
1⅓ c flour
1 tsp baking powder
2 Tbsp unsweetened cocoa powder

For the filling
7 oz caramel-flavored baking chocolate
½ c whipping cream

For the icing
1 c confectioner's sugar
1 c whipping cream
¼ c salted butter

Make the cakes. Preheat the oven to 350°. Melt the baking chocolate and the butter together over low heat. In a mixing bowl, mix together the sugar and the eggs, then add the melted butter and chocolate; mix well. Add the flour, baking powder, and cocoa and mix everything together. Place the batter in small circles on a baking sheet. Bake for 10 minutes. When the cakes are done, remove them from the heat and let them cool.

Prepare the chocolate-caramel filling. Break the caramel-flavored chocolate into small pieces and place them in a mixing bowl. Heat the whipping cream, then pour it over the chocolate. Mix well, then let chill for several minutes. Spread the filling on half of the cakes, then put the plain and iced cakes together.

Prepare the salted butter caramel icing. Spread the confectioner's sugar evenly over the bottom of a frying pan and let it sit, without stirring, over medium heat until the sugar turns a light caramel color. Remove from the heat and add the whipping cream gradually. Put the mixture back on the stove and heat for 1 or 2 minutes, stirring constantly. Remove it from the heat again and add the butter, still stirring. Let the mixture cool, then spread it over the tops of the assembled whoopie pies.

Cookie butter is the American version of European Biscoff Spread (also called Speculoos Spread), made from spicy, sugary cookies. You can find this spread in most grocery stores.

Cookie-butter whoopie pies

MAKES 20 WHOOPIE PIES ABOUT
1 IN. IN DIAMETER

PREPARATION: 25 MIN

COOKING: 8 MIN

For the cakes

½ c butter, softened

⅔ c sugar

3 eggs

2 c flour

2 tsp cinnamon

1 tsp baking powder

½ tsp baking soda

2 oz crushed gingersnaps
(or other spicy cookies)

For the filling

¾ c cookie-butter spread, plus
¼ c for the topping

7 oz mascarpone

Make the cakes. Preheat the oven to 350º. Put the butter and sugar in a mixing bow and beat with an electric mixer until the mixture turns white. Add the eggs one at a time, beating after each egg is added. Sift in the flour, cinnamon, baking powder, and baking soda. Beat on medium speed for 1 to 2 minutes; the batter should become smooth and all the ingredients should be mixed in completely. Add the crushed cookies to the mixture. Place the batter in small circles on a baking sheet. Bake for 8 minutes, then let cool.

Make the cookie-butter cream. In a mixing bowl, beat the cookie-butter spread and mascarpone into a smooth cream. Use a small spoon to spread the cream on the flat sides of half of the cakes, then put the iced and plain cakes together.

Decorate the whoopie pies. Melt the reserved cookie-butter spread by putting it in the microwave for several seconds. Drizzle this over the whoopie pies. Sprinkle a few crumbs of crushed cookies over them.

Variation: Decorate your whoopie pies with colored sprinkles.

Peanut butter and caramel whoopie pies

MAKES 20 WHOOPIE PIES ABOUT
1 IN. IN DIAMETER

PREPARATION: 35 MIN

COOKING: 8 MIN

REFRIGERATION: 30 MIN

For the cakes
⅔ c butter, softened
⅔ c sugar
3 eggs
2 c flour
1 tsp vanilla extract
1 tsp baking powder
1 tsp baking soda

For the filling
1 c butter, softened
1⅓ c confectioner's sugar
1 c peanut butter

For the caramel sauce
½ c whipping cream
12 chewy caramel candies

Make the cakes. Preheat the oven to 350º. In a mixing bowl, beat the butter and sugar together until the mixture turns white. Add the eggs one at a time, mixing after adding each egg, then add the vanilla extract. Sift in the flour, baking powder, and baking soda. Beat on medium speed for 1 to 2 minutes; the batter should be smooth and all the ingredients mixed in completely. Place the batter in small circles on a baking sheet. Bake for 8 minutes, then let cool.

Make the peanut butter cream. In a mixing bowl, beat the butter and confectioner's sugar together into a smooth, creamy mixture. Add the peanut butter and beat for 1 minute to obtain a light, fluffy cream. Chill in the refrigerator for 30 minutes.

Prepare the caramel sauce. Pour the cream into a saucepan. Add the caramels and heat over low heat, stirring with a whisk, until the candy melts. Let cool to room temperature.

Use a pastry bag or small spoon to spread the peanut butter cream on the flat sides of half of the cakes. Put the iced cakes and plain cakes together. Put a bit of peanut butter cream on the tops of the whoopie pies. Drizzle the cooled caramel sauce over the whoopie pies immediately before serving.

Chocolate-hazelnut spread whoopie pies

MAKES 15 WHOOPIE PIES ABOUT
1 IN. IN DIAMETER

PREPARATION: 15 MIN

COOKING: 10 MIN

For the cakes

½ c butter, softened

⅔ c sugar

2 eggs

1½ c flour

1 tsp baking powder

½ tsp baking soda

¼ c unsweetened cocoa powder

For the filling

1 c chocolate-hazelnut spread
(such as Nutella)

Make the cakes. Preheat the oven to 350°. In a mixing bowl, beat the butter and sugar together until the mixture turns white. Add the eggs one at a time, mixing after adding each egg. Sift in the flour, baking powder, baking soda, and cocoa powder. Beat on medium speed for 1 to 2 minutes; the batter should be smooth and all the ingredients mixed in completely. Place the batter in small circles on a baking sheet. Bake for 10 minutes, then let cool.

Fill the whoopie pies. Spread chocolate-hazelnut spread on the flat sides of half the cakes, then put the filled cakes and plain cakes together. Top with a little more spread. You can garnish the whoopie pies with chopped nuts.

Triple chocolate whoopie pies

MAKES 15 WHOOPIE PIES ABOUT
1 IN. IN DIAMETER

PREPARATION: 35 MIN

COOKING: 10 MIN

For the cakes

2 oz bittersweet or dark baking chocolate (at least 67% cacao)

⅓ c butter, softened

½ c sugar

2 eggs

1⅓ c flour

1 tsp baking powder

2 Tbsp unsweetened cocoa powder

For the filling

7 oz white baking chocolate

⅔ c whipping cream

For the icing

3 oz milk chocolate or semisweet baking chocolate

2 Tbsp whipping cream

Make the cakes. Preheat the oven to 350°. In a saucepan, melt the baking chocolate and the butter together over low heat. In a mixing bowl, beat the sugar and eggs together until the mixture turns white. Add the chocolate-butter mixture, and mix well. Add the flour, baking powder, and cocoa powder, and mix well. Place the batter in small circles on a baking sheet. Bake for 10 minutes, then let cool.

Make the filling. Cut or break the white chocolate into small pieces in a mixing bowl. Heat the whipping cream, then pour it over the chocolate. Stir until you obtain a smooth, shiny chocolate. Let chill for several minutes, then spread the filling on the flat sides of half the cakes. Put the filled cakes and plain cakes together.

Make the icing. Chop the milk chocolate and place it in a mixing bowl. Heat the whipping cream, then pour it over the chocolate. Stir until you obtain a smooth, shiny chocolate. Let chill, then spread it on the tops of the whoopie pies.

The rich taste of chestnuts makes these desserts distinctly different!

Chestnut cream whoopie pies

MAKES 20 WHOOPIE PIES ABOUT
1 IN. IN DIAMETER

PREPARATION: 20 MIN

COOKING: 8 MIN

For the cakes

½ c butter, softened

½ c sugar

3 eggs

2⅓ c flour

1 Tbsp vanilla extract

1 tsp baking powder

½ tsp baking soda

For the filling

8 oz mascarpone

¾ c chestnut cream
(chestnut puree)*

1 tsp vanilla extract

*Note: If you can't find chestnut cream, make your own. Soften peeled chestnuts in lightly simmering milk for 15 minutes. Then puree them, adding a bit of milk as needed.

Make the cakes. Preheat the oven to 350°. In a mixing bowl, beat the butter and sugar together until the mixture turns white. Add the eggs one at a time, mixing after adding each egg, then add the vanilla extract. Sift in the flour, baking powder, and baking soda. Beat on medium speed for 1 to 2 minutes; the batter should be smooth and all the ingredients mixed in completely. Place the batter in small circles on a baking sheet. Bake for 8 minutes, then let cool.

Make the filling. Beat the mascarpone, chestnut cream, and vanilla extract with an electric mixer until the mixture is smooth, creamy, and fluffy.

Fill the whoopie pies. Use a spoon or spatula to spread the filling on the flat sides of half of the cakes, then put the iced cakes and plain cakes together. Garnish the tops with the remaining chestnut cream.

Variation: You can decorate these whoopie pies with a bit of melted chocolate or colored sprinkles.

Tiramisu whoopie pies

MAKES 15 TO 20 WHOOPIE PIES
ABOUT 1 IN. IN DIAMETER

PREPARATION: 30 MIN

COOKING: 8 MIN

REFRIGERATION: 2 HRS

For the cakes

½ c butter, softened

½ c sugar

3 eggs

2⅓ c flour

1 tsp coffee extract*

1 tsp baking powder

½ tsp baking soda

For the filling

1 whole egg + 1 egg yolk

⅓ c sugar

8 oz mascarpone

1 Tbsp amaretto (optional)

¼ c cocoa powder

*Note: You can make your own coffee extract by carmelizing 1 c of sugar and adding ½ c of hot espresso or very strong coffee. Carefully carmelize the sugar a little at a time in a nonstick pan over medium heat. Then remove from heat and add the espresso gradually, stirring well.

Make the cakes. Preheat the oven to 350°. In a mixing bowl, beat the butter and sugar together until the mixture turns white. Add the eggs one at a time, mixing after adding each egg, then add the coffee extract. Sift in the flour, baking powder, and baking soda. Beat on medium speed for 1 to 2 minutes; the batter should be smooth and all the ingredients mixed in completely. Place the batter in small circles on a baking sheet. Bake for 8 minutes, then let cool.

Make the filling. Separate the white and the yolk of the whole egg. In a mixing bowl, beat the two egg yolks and confectioner's sugar until the mixture turns white. Add the mascarpone, and then the amaretto, if desired. Beat until the mixture is smooth and creamy. Beat the egg white until peaks are formed, then add the beaten egg white to the filling and mix well. Chill in the refrigerator for at least 2 hours.

Fill the whoopie pies. Use a spoon or spatula to spread the filling on the flat sides of half of the cakes, then put the iced cakes and the plain cakes together. Put a little bit of the filling on top of each whoopie pie as decoration, and sprinkle cocoa powder over the tops.

The pairing of chocolate and orange is absolutely delicious. A whoopie pie that combines the two flavors is guaranteed to please!

Chocolate and orange whoopie pies

MAKES ABOUT 15 WHOOPIE PIES

PREPARATION: 25 MIN

COOKING: 10 MIN

For the cakes

½ c butter, softened

⅔ c sugar

2 eggs

1½ c flour

1 tsp baking powder

½ tsp baking soda

¼ c unsweetened cocoa powder

1 oz candied orange peels*, chopped

For the filling

¾ c milk

1 vanilla bean

2 egg yolks

⅓ c confectioner's sugar

5 Tbsp cornstarch

1 Tbsp orange liquer (triple sec)

For the icing

3 oz semisweet or bittersweet baking chocolate

2 Tbsp whipping cream

Make the cakes. Preheat the oven to 350º. In a mixing bowl, beat the butter and sugar together until the mixture turns white. Add the eggs one at a time, mixing after adding each egg. Sift in the flour, baking powder, baking soda, and cocoa powder. Beat on medium speed for 1 minute. Mix the candied orange peels into the batter. Place the batter in small circles on a baking sheet. Bake for 10 minutes, then let cool.

Make the filling. Heat the milk in a saucepan over low heat. Cut the vanilla bean in half and add it (including the seeds) to the milk. In a mixing bowl, beat the eggs and sugar, then add the cornstarch and mix well. When the milk is hot, pour half of it into the egg mixture. Mix well, then pour the whole mixture into the saucepan. Keep over low heat, stirring constantly, until the mixture thickens. Take the cream off the heat, add the liquer, mix well, and then put it in the refrigerator to cool. When it has cooled, spread the mixture on the flat sides of half of the cakes, then put the iced cakes and plain cakes together.

Make the icing. Break the chocolate into small pieces and place them in a mixing bowl. Heat the cream in the microwave, then pour it over the cocolate. Mix until all the chocolate has melted, then let the mixture cool. Spread it on the tops of the pies.

*Note: To candy your own orange peels, boil ¼-inch slices of orange peels in water for about 15 minutes, then drain and rinse. Add them to a boiling mixture of 1 part water and 1 part sugar, reduce heat, and simmer until the pieces are soft (at least ½ hour). Remove the peels, coat them with sugar, then let them dry completely.

To make this recipe, you need classic almond pralines—or, if you can find it, the French candy known as Pralinoise.

Praline whoopie pies

MAKES 20 WHOOPIE PIES ABOUT
1 IN. IN DIAMETER

PREPARATION: 30 MIN

COOOKING: 8 MIN

For the cakes
½ c butter, softened
½ c sugar
3 eggs
2⅓ c flour
1 tsp baking powder
1 tsp baking soda
2 oz almond pralines (or Pralinoise)

For the filling
11 oz semisweet chocolate
½ c whipping cream
1½ Tbsp butter

For the decoration
5¼ oz cream cheese
⅔ c confectioner's sugar

Make the cakes. Preheat the oven to 350°. In a mixing bowl, beat the butter and sugar together until the mixture turns white. Add the eggs one at a time, mixing after adding each egg. Sift in the flour, baking powder, and baking soda. Beat on medium speed for 1 to 2 minutes. Crush the pralines finely and mix them into the batter. Place the batter in small circles on a baking sheet. Bake for 8 minutes, then let cool.

Make the filling. Cut the chocolate into pieces and place it in a microwave-safe mixing bowl, along with the whipping cream. Microwave the chocolate and cream for 1 minute. Mix with a whisk until the mixture is smooth and shiny. Add the butter and mix well. Place in the refrigerator until the mixture is stiff enough to spread. Use a spoon or a pastry bag to put the filling on the flat sides of half of the cakes, then put the iced cakes and plain cakes together.

Decorate the whoopie pies. Beat the cream cheese and confectioner's sugar with an electric mixer. Put a little bit of this mixture on top of each whoopie pie, then sprinkle on the remaining crushed pralines.

Cookie whoopie pies

MAKES 20 WHOOPIE PIES ABOUT
1 IN. IN DIAMETER

PREPARATION: 25 MIN

COOKING: 8 MIN

For the cakes

½ c butter, softened

½ c sugar

3 eggs

2⅓ c flour

1 tsp baking powder

1 tsp baking soda

5 oz dark chocolate chunks

⅓ c hazelnuts or peanuts, unsalted
and chopped

For the filling

5 oz milk chocolate or semisweet
baking chocolate

½ c whipping cream

Make the cakes. Preheat the oven to 350°. In a mixing bowl, beat the butter and sugar together until the mixture turns white. Add the eggs one at a time, mixing after adding each egg. Sift in the flour, baking powder, and baking soda. Beat on medium speed for 1 to 2 minutes; the batter should be smooth and all the ingredients mixed in completely. Place the batter in small circles on a baking sheet, then press the chocolate chunks and nuts into the batter. Bake for 8 minutes, then let cool.

Make the chocolate filling. Chop the chocolate into small pieces and place them in a mixing bowl. Heat the cream, then pour it over the chocolate. Mix until the chocolate is smooth and shiny. Refrigerate for several minutes, until the filling is stiff enough to spread. Use a spoon or spatula to spread the filling on half the cakes, then put the iced cakes and plain cakes together.

The combination of banana, chocolate, and caramel is impossible to resist! You can replace the dulce de leche with homemade salted butter caramel (recipe on page 8).

Banana toffee whoopie pies

MAKES 25 WHOOPIE PIES ABOUT 1 IN. IN DIAMETER

PREPARATION: 35 MIN

COOKING: 8 MIN

For the cakes
- ½ c butter, softened
- ⅔ c sugar
- 3 eggs
- 2⅓ c flour
- 1 tsp baking powder
- 1 tsp baking soda
- 2 bananas

For the filling
- 3 or 4 bananas
- 3 Tbsp lemon juice
- 5 oz bittersweet or dark baking chocolate (at least 67% cacao)
- 4 Tbsp milk
- 1½ Tbsp cold whipping cream
- 5 Tbsp dulce de leche

Make the cakes. Preheat the oven to 350°. In a mixing bowl, beat the butter and sugar together until the mixture turns white. Add the eggs one at a time, mixing after adding each egg. Sift in the flour, baking powder, and baking soda. Beat on medium speed for 1 to 2 minutes; the batter should be smooth and all the ingredients mixed in completely. Mash the bananas, then add them to the batter and mix well. Place the batter in small circles on a baking sheet. Bake for 8 minutes, then let cool.

Make the filling. Cut the bananas into thin slices, then drizzle them with lemon juice so they don't brown. Chop the chocolate and place it in a microwave-safe bowl, along with the milk. Microwave it for 1 minute, then mix until the chocolate mixture is smooth and shiny. If necessary, microwave it for a few more seconds so the chocolate is melted and mixed in completely. Beat the chilled cream into whipped cream.

Fill the whoopie pies. Place several banana slices on the flat side of half of the cakes. Spread a bit of the melted chocolate over the bananas, then add a bit of dulce de leche. Top with the remaining cakes.

Decorate the whoopie pies with whipped cream and a slice of banana. Eat immediately—the whipped cream will not wait for you!

For an even more flavorful apricot cream, add a vanilla pod cut in two when you simmer the fruit. You can also replace the sesame seeds with lavender.

Apricot and sesame whoopie pies

MAKES 20 WHOOPIE PIES ABOUT
1 IN. IN DIAMETER

PREPARATION: 25 MIN

COOKING: 8 MIN

For the cakes
½ c butter, softened
⅔ c sugar
3 eggs
2 c flour
1 tsp baking powder
1 tsp baking soda
2 tsp sesame seeds

For the filling
1½ c apricots, quartered
¼ c sugar
1 tsp vanilla extract
8 oz mascarpone

Make the cakes. Preheat the oven to 350°. In a mixing bowl, beat the butter and sugar together until the mixture turns white. Add the eggs one at a time, mixing after adding each egg. Sift in the flour, baking powder, and baking soda. Beat on medium speed for 1 to 2 minutes; the batter should be smooth and all the ingredients mixed in completely. Add the sesame seeds and mix them in. Place the batter in small circles on a baking sheet. Bake for 8 minutes, then let cool.

Make the apricot cream. Put 1 Tbsp water in a saucepan. Add the apricots, sugar, and vanilla. Simmer over low heat until the apricots are soft and the mixture has thickened. Let cool, then blend thoroughly. Beat the mascarpone, then add it to the apricot puree gradually, mixing constantly. Beat well to obtain a smooth and even texture. Spread the cream on the flat sides of half the cakes and put them together with the remaining cakes.

Decorate the whoopie pies. Spread a little bit of apricot cream on top and garnish with a few sprinkles or a thin slice of fruit.

Coconut whoopie pies

MAKES 20 WHOOPIE PIES ABOUT
1 IN. IN DIAMETER

PREPARATION: 30 MIN

COOKING: 8 MIN

For the cakes

½ c butter, softened

⅔ c sugar

3 eggs

2 c flour

1 tsp baking powder

½ tsp baking soda

½ c shredded coconut

the zest of 1 lime

For the filling

8 oz mascarpone

¼ c coconut milk

⅔ c confectioner's sugar

1¼ c shredded coconut

1 egg white

For the icing

½ an egg white

1 c confectioner's sugar

a few drops of lime juice

Make the cakes. Preheat the oven to 350°. In a mixing bowl, beat the butter and sugar together until the mixture turns white. Add the eggs one at a time, mixing after adding each egg. Sift in the flour, baking powder, and baking soda. Beat on medium speed for 3 to 4 minutes; the batter should be smooth and all the ingredients mixed in completely. Add the shredded coconut and lime zest and mix well. Place the batter in small circles on a baking sheet. Bake for 8 minutes, then let cool.

Make the coconut cream. In a mixing bowl, beat the mascarpone and gradually add half the coconut milk. Beat the mixture until creamy, then add the confectioner's sugar and shredded coconut. Add the rest of the coconut milk. Beat the egg white until stiff peaks form, then fold it into the mixture, mixing just enough to incorporate all the ingredients. Use a small spoon to spread the cream on the flat sides of half the cakes, then put the iced cakes and plain cakes together.

Make the icing. Beat the egg white and confectioner's sugar to obtain a smooth, shiny mixture; add several drops of lime juice and beat again. Use a small spoon to spread the icing on the tops of the assembled whoopie pies.

If the blueberry jam you use contains large pieces of fruit, crush them with a fork; otherwise, the pieces can block the opening of your pastry bag.

Blueberry whoopie pies

MAKES 20 WHOOPIE PIES ABOUT
1 IN. IN DIAMETER

PREPARATION: 25 MIN

COOKING: 8 MIN

For the cakes
- ½ c butter, softened
- ⅓ c sugar
- ⅓ c brown sugar, packed
- 2 eggs
- 1⅓ c flour
- ¼ c almonds, finely ground
- 1 tsp baking powder
- ½ tsp baking soda
- 2 Tbsp blueberry jam

For the filling
- 14 oz cream cheese
- ½ c butter, softened
- 1 c confectioner's sugar
- 2 Tbsp blueberry jam

Make the cakes. Preheat the oven to 350º. In a mixing bowl, beat the butter, sugar, and brown sugar together until the mixture turns white. Add the eggs one at a time, mixing after adding each egg. Sift in the flour, almonds, baking powder, and baking soda. Beat on medium speed for 1 minute; the batter should be smooth and all the ingredients mixed in completely. Add the blueberry jam and mix gently. Place the batter in small circles on a baking sheet. Bake for 8 minutes, then let cool.

Make the filling. Combine the cream cheese, butter, and confectioner's sugar and beat with an electric mixer for 2 minutes, until the mixture is smooth and creamy. Add the jam and beat again. Use a spoon or pastry bag to put a bit of the cream on the flat sides of half of the cakes, then assemble the whoopies.

Decorate the tops of the whoopie pies with a bit of the leftover cream.

Tip: Place a fresh blueberry on top of each whoopie pie.

Pistachio butter is the key to this recipe: Its flavor is incomparable. You can find it in gourmet grocery stores, Asian groceries, or online. You can also use this ingredient in other deserts—creme brule, macaroons, panna cottas . . . yum!

Pistachio whoopie pies

MAKES 20 WHOOPIE PIES ABOUT 1 IN. IN DIAMETER

PREPARATION: 40 MIN

COOKING: 8 MIN

For the cakes
- ½ c butter, softened
- ½ c sugar
- 3 eggs
- 2⅓ c flour
- 1 tsp baking powder
- 1 tsp baking soda
- 1 tsp rose water

For the filling
- 1 c milk
- 2 egg yolks
- ⅓ c confectioner's sugar
- 5 Tbsp cornstarch
- 1 Tbsp pistachio butter

For the icing
- ½ egg yolk
- 1 c confectioner's sugar
- a few drops of rose water

Make the cakes. Preheat the oven to 350°. In a mixing bowl, beat the butter and sugar together until the mixture turns white. Add the eggs one at a time, mixing after adding each egg. Sift in the flour, baking powder, baking soda, and rose water. Beat on medium speed for 1 to 2 minutes. Place the batter in small circles on a baking sheet. Bake for 8 minutes, then let cool.

Make the pistachio filling. Heat the milk in a saucepan. Beat the egg yolks and confectioner's sugar until the mixture turns white. Add the cornstarch and mix well. When the milk is hot, pour half of it into the egg mixture. Mix well, then pour the entire egg mixture into the saucepan with the rest of the milk. Place the saucepan back on the stove and stir constantly, until the mixture thickens. Remove from the heat and let cool. Add the pistachio butter, mix again, and place in the refrigerator to chill. Spread the cream on the flat slides of half of the cakes, then put the iced cakes and plain cakes together.

Make the icing. Beat the egg white and the confectioner's sugar, then add the rose water. Mix well, then spread the icing on the tops of the assembled whoopie pies.

Tip: Add a bit of red food coloring to the icing. Decorate the whoopie pies with chopped pistachios.

Ice cream and pecan whoopie pies

MAKES 20 WHOOPIE PIES ABOUT
1 IN. IN DIAMETER

PREPARATION: 20 MIN

COOKING: 8 MIN

For the cakes

½ c butter, softened

½ c sugar

3 eggs

2 c flour

1 tsp vanilla extract

1 tsp baking powder

1 tsp baking soda

For the filling

14 oz vanilla ice cream

For the topping

7 oz mascarpone

⅛ c confectioner's sugar

1 egg white

½ c caramel sauce

about 20 pecans (optional)

Make the cakes. Preheat the oven to 350º. In a mixing bowl, beat the butter and sugar together until the mixture turns white. Add the eggs one at a time, mixing after adding each egg, then add the vanilla extract. Sift in the flour, baking powder, and baking soda. Beat on medium speed for 1 to 2 minutes; the batter should be smooth and all the ingredients mixed in completely. Place the batter in small circles on a baking sheet. Bake for 8 minutes, then let cool.

Make the topping. Beat the mascarpone and confectioner's sugar together. Beat the egg white until stiff peaks form, then add it to the mixture, mixing until the toppping is smooth and creamy.

Fill the whoopie pies. Let the ice cream soften a bit before spreading it on the flat sides of half the cakes, then put them together with the other half of the cakes. Spread a bit of the mascarpone cream on the top of each assembled whoopie pie, and drizzle caramel sauce on top of the cream. Serve immediately.

Idea: Add a pecan on top of each whoopie pie.

Tip: If the caramel sauce is not thin enough, place the jar in a saucepan with a little water and heat it slightly. If it is too thin, place it in the freezer for a while to stiffen up.

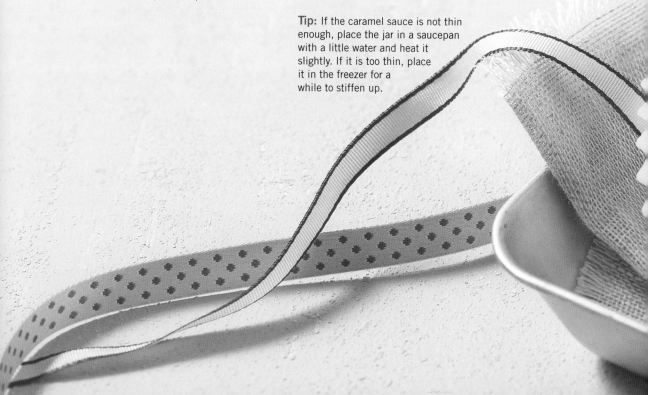

When whipping cream, don't forget to put the cream in the refrigerator at least 2 hours before whipping it: It should be around 40°. And you can put your bowl and beaters in the freezer a few minutes beforehand, too.

Strawberry-basil whoopie pies

MAKES 20 WHOOPIE PIES ABOUT
1 IN. IN DIAMETER

PREPARATION: 30 MIN

COOKING: 8 MIN

For the cakes

½ c butter, softened

½ c sugar

3 eggs

2 c flour

1 tsp vanilla extract

1 tsp baking powder

1 tsp baking soda

several fresh basil leaves

For the filling

1¼ c strawberries, plus 7 or 8 for garnishes

1¼ c whipping cream

⅛ c confectioner's sugar

Make the cakes. Preheat the oven to 350°. In a mixing bowl, beat the butter and sugar together until the mixture turns white. Add the eggs one at a time, mixing after adding each egg, then add the vanilla extract. Sift in the flour, baking powder, and baking soda. Beat on medium speed for 1 to 2 minutes; the batter should be smooth and all the ingredients mixed in completely. Chop the basil finely and add it to the batter. Place the batter in small circles on a baking sheet. Bake for 8 minutes, then let cool.

Make the strawberry whipped cream. Wash the strawberries and remove the leaves, then puree the berries in a blender. Set this aside. Pour the well-chilled whipping cream in a bowl and whip it into whipped cream with an electric mixer. Before it gets too stiff, add the sugar. When the whipped cream is nice and stiff, fold in the pureed strawberries. Use a pastry bag with a fluted tip to put strawberry cream on the flat sides of half of the cakes. Put the iced cakes and the plain cakes together.

Decorate the whoopie pies with a bit of leftover whipped cream. Cut the remaining strawberries into thin slices and place one on each whoopie.

These tiny whoopie pies will make a big impression at a dinner party or chic picnic!

Lavender whoopie pies

MAKES 30 WHOOPIE PIES ABOUT ¾ IN. IN DIAMETER

PREPARATION: 30 MIN

COOKING: 8 MIN

REFRIGERATION: 1 HR

For the cakes

½ c butter, softened

½ c sugar

3 eggs

2⅓ c flour

1 tsp dried lavender

1 tsp baking powder

½ tsp baking soda

purple food coloring (optional)

For the filling

¾ c lychees in syrup*

7 oz mascarpone

⅛ c confectioner's sugar

1 egg white

For the icing

½ the white of 1 egg

1 c confectioner's sugar

Make the cakes. Preheat the oven to 350°. In a mixing bowl, beat the butter and sugar together until the mixture turns white. Add the eggs one at a time, mixing after adding each egg. Sift in the flour, baking powder, and baking soda. Once the dry ingredients are mixed in, add the food coloring, if desired. Beat on medium speed for 1 to 2 minutes; the batter should be smooth and all the ingredients mixed in completely. Place the batter in small circles on a baking sheet. Bake for 8 minutes, then let cool.

Make the lychee cream. Drain the lychees over a mixing bowl, saving 2 Tbsp of the syrup. Cut the fruits into very small pieces; set aside. In a mixing bowl, beat the mascarpone and confectioner's sugar. Beat the egg white separately until stiff peaks form, then add this to the mascarpone mixture. When the mixture is very smooth, add the chopped lychees. Chill the mixture in the refrigerator for 1 hour.

Prepare the icing. Beat the egg white and confectioner's sugar. Add the reserved lychee syrup.

Spread the lychee cream on the flat sides of half the cakes; put the plain cakes and the iced ones together, and top with icing.

*Note: Lychees are unique, sweet fruits easily found in the Asian section of a grocery store.

Raspberry whoopie pies

MAKES 20 WHOOPIE PIES ABOUT
1 IN. IN DIAMETER

PREPARATION: 30 MIN

COOKING: 8 MIN

For the cakes

⅔ c butter, softened

⅔ c sugar

3 eggs

2 c flour

1 tsp vanilla extract

1 tsp baking powder

1 tsp baking soda

For the filling

1¾ c milk

1 vanilla bean

2 egg yolks

⅓ c cornstarch

For garnishing

3 c raspberries

Make the cakes. Preheat the oven to 350°. In a mixing bowl, beat the butter and sugar together until the mixture turns white. Add the eggs one at a time, mixing after adding each egg, then add the vanilla extract. Sift in the flour, baking powder, and baking soda. Beat on medium speed for 1 to 2 minutes; the batter should be smooth and all the ingredients mixed in completely. Place the batter in small circles on a baking sheet. Bake for 8 minutes, then let cool.

Make the vanilla cream. Pour the milk in a saucepan and place over low heat; add the vanilla bean, cut in half. While the milk is heating, beat the egg yolks and the sugar in a mixing bowl until the mixture becomes white. Add the cornstarch and mix well. When the milk is hot, pour half of it into the egg mixture. Mix, then pour this mixture back into the saucepan with the rest of the milk. Cook over low heat, stirring constantly, until the mixture thickens. Let the cream chill.

Use a small spoon or a pastry bag to spread cream on the flat sides of half of the cakes. Place several raspberries on the cream, then place a plain cake on top. Garnish with a little bit of cream and one more raspberry.

Marshmallow whoopie pies

MAKES 20 WHOOPIE PIES ABOUT
1 IN. IN DIAMETER

PREPARATION: 20 MIN

COOKING: 8 MIN

For the cakes

½ c butter, softened

½ c sugar

3 eggs

2⅓ c flour

1 tsp vanilla extract

1 tsp baking powder

½ tsp baking soda

For the filling

1 c butter, softened

2¼ c confectioner's sugar

30 large marshmallows

Make the cakes. Preheat the oven to 350°. In a mixing bowl, beat the butter and sugar together until the mixture turns white. Add the eggs one at a time, mixing after adding each egg, then add the vanilla extract. Sift in the flour, baking powder, and baking soda. Beat on medium speed for 1 to 2 minutes; the batter should be smooth and all the ingredients mixed in completely. Place the batter in small circles on a baking sheet. Bake for 8 minutes, then let cool.

Make the marshmallow filling. Beat the butter and confectioner's sugar until the mixture is fluffy. In a saucepan, carefully melt the marshmallows over very low heat, with a little bit of water. Stir the marshmallows constantly, and if it seems like they are sticking to the bottom, take them off the heat. Pour the melted marsh-mallows into the butter-sugar mixture. Mix well, until the mixture is fluffy. Spread the filling on the flat sides of half of the cakes, then put the iced cakes and plain cakes together.

Decorate the tops of the whoopie pies with the rest of the marshmallow cream.

Idea: Add mini marshmallows, chopped walnuts, and mini chocolate chips on top.

These whoopie pies are very easy to make and a delightful summertime treat.

Lemon meringue whoopie pies

MAKES 20 WHOOPIE PIES ABOUT 1 IN. IN DIAMETER

PREPARATION: 10 MIN

COOKING: 8 MIN

For the cakes
½ c butter, softened
⅔ c sugar
3 eggs
2 c flour
the zest of 1 lemon, finely grated
½ tsp lemon extract
1 tsp baking powder
1 tsp baking soda

For the filling
1 jar of lemon curd

For the meringue
2 egg whites
1 c confectioner's sugar

Make the cakes. Preheat the oven to 350°. In a mixing bowl, beat the butter and sugar together until the mixture turns white. Add the eggs one at a time, mixing after adding each egg, then add the lemon extract. Sift in the flour, baking powder, and baking soda, then add the lemon zest. Beat on medium speed for 1 to 2 minutes; the batter should be smooth and all the ingredients mixed in completely. Place the batter in small circles on a baking sheet. Bake for 8 minutes, then let cool.

Make the meringue. Turn your oven's broiler to medium. Beat the egg whites until stiff peaks form. Place the mixing bowl with the egg whites on top of a saucepan of boiling water to make a double-boiler. Mix the egg whites with a spatula for 5 minutes without stopping. They should become shiny.

Spread lemon curd on the flat sides of half of the cakes, then put a bit of meringue on the round sides of the other half of the cakes. Place the cakes with the meringue in the oven under the broiler, on the middle rack, until the meringue turns golden brown (1 to 2 minutes). Remove from the oven and let cool to room temperature. Put the cakes with the meringue and the cakes with the lemon curd together.

This birthday whoopie pie can be stored in the refrigerator for up to 24 hours; in this case, don't make the meringue until the last minute.

Birthday whoopie pie

MAKES 1 WHOOPIE PIE ABOUT
8 IN. IN DIAMETER

PREPARATION: 40 MIN

COOKING: 12 TO 15 MIN

For the cakes
⅔ c butter, softened
⅔ c sugar
3 eggs
1⅔ c flour
2 Tbsp almonds, finely ground
1 tsp vanilla extract
1 tsp baking powder
1 tsp baking soda

For the filling
11 oz milk chocolate or semisweet
baking chocolate
¾ c whipping cream

For the meringue
2 egg whites
1 c confectioner' sugar

Make the cakes. Preheat the oven to 350°. In a mixing bowl, beat the butter and sugar together until the mixture turns white. Add the eggs one at a time, mixing after adding each egg, then add the vanilla extract. Sift in the flour, baking powder, and baking soda, then add the almonds. Beat on medium speed for 1 to 2 minutes. Divide the batter in half. Put a sheet of parchment paper on a baking sheet and draw two 6-inch circles on it; leave plenty of space between the circles. Pour the batter onto each circle and bake for 12 to 15 minutes. Let cool.

Make the chocolate filling. Chop the chocolate and place it in a mixing bowl. Heat the cream and pour it over the chocolate pieces. Mix until the chocolate mixture is smooth and shiny. Put the filling in the refrigerator to chill.

Make the meringue. Turn on your oven's broiler. Beat the egg whites in a mixing bowl until stiff peaks form. Put the bowl on top of a saucepan of boiling water to make a double boiler. Mix the egg whites constantly for 5 minutes.

Spread the filling on the flat side of one of the cakes. Spread the meringue on the round side of the other cake. Place the cake with the meringue on the middle rack of the oven under the broiler until the meringue turns golden brown (1 to 2 minutes). Put the two halves of the whoopie pie together.

Instead of round, this whoopie is heart shaped: ideal for Valentine's Day or an anniversary. You can experiment with cookie cutters of any shape—stars for Christmas, for example.

Whoopie pies à la rose

MAKES ABOUT 15 WHOOPIE PIES

PREPARATION: 25 MIN

COOKING: 10 TO 12 MIN, DEPENDING ON THE SIZE OF THE WHOOPIE PIES

For the cakes

½ c butter, softened

1⅓ c confectioner's sugar

2 eggs

1⅓ c flour

½ c almonds, finely ground

1 tsp baking powder

½ tsp baking soda

12 Jordan almonds, crushed

For the filling

8 oz cream cheese

½ c butter, softened

1 c confectioner's sugar

2 Tbsp rose water

For the icing

½ an egg white

1 c confectioner's sugar

several drops of rose water

Make the cakes. Preheat the oven to 350°. In a mixing bowl, beat the butter and sugar together until the mixture turns white. Add the eggs one at a time, mixing after adding each egg. Sift in the flour, baking powder, and baking soda, then add the plain almonds. Beat on medium speed for 3 to 4 minutes; the batter should be smooth and all the ingredients mixed in completely. Add the Jordan almonds to the batter in two stages. Place a sheet of parchment paper on a baking sheet and place the batter on it in circles a little bit larger than the cookie cutter you plan to use. Bake for 10 to 12 minutes, then let cool. Use the cookie cutter to cut shapes from the cakes.

Make the filling. Beat the cream cheese, butter, confectioner's sugar, and rose water with an electric mixer for 2 minutes, until the mixture is smooth and creamy. Use a small spoon or a pastry bag to spread the filling on half of the cakes, then put the plain cakes and iced cakes together.

Make the icing. Beat the egg white and confectioner's sugar until the mixture is smooth and shiny. Add several drops of rose water, then beat again. Use a small spoon to spread the icing on the tops of the whoopie pies.

Decorate the whoopie pies with any leftover ground Jordans. You can eat these whoopie pies right away or keep them in the refrigerator for up to 48 hours.

Here is a delicious carrot-cake–style whoopie pie with cream cheese filling, perfect for a weekend brunch.

Carrot cake whoopie pies

MAKES 25 WHOOPIE PIES ABOUT
1 IN. IN DIAMETER

PREPARATION: 25 MIN

COOKING: 8 MIN

REFRIGERATION: 30 MIN

For the cakes

½ c butter, softened

⅔ c sugar

3 eggs

2 c flour

2 tsp cinnamon

1 tsp baking powder

½ tsp baking soda

¾ c carrots, finely grated

¼ c chopped pecans or walnuts

For the filling

6 Tbsp butter, softened

10 oz cream cheese

2 c confectioner's sugar

1 tsp vanilla extract

Make the cakes. Preheat the oven to 350°. In a mixing bowl, beat the butter and sugar together until the mixture turns white. Add the eggs one at a time, mixing after adding each egg. Sift in the flour, baking powder, baking soda, and cinnamon. Beat on medium speed for 1 to 2 minutes; the batter should be smooth and all the ingredients mixed in completely. Add the carrots and nuts and mix well. Place the batter in small circles on a baking sheet. Bake for 8 minutes, then let cool.

Make the cream cheese filling. In a mixing bowl, beat together the butter and cream cheese until they are thoroughly combined, then add the confectioner's sugar and vanilla. Beat for 1 to 2 minutes until the cream is light and fluffy. Chill in the refrigerator for at least 30 minutes. Use a small spoon to spread the cream cheese frosting on the flat sides of half of the cakes, then put the plain cakes and filled cakes together. Put the rest of the frosting in a pastry bag and use it to decorate the tops of the whoopie pies.

Idea: Decorate the whoopie pies with colored sprinkles.

Tomato and tapenade whoopie pies

MAKES 20 WHOOPIE PIES ABOUT
1 IN. IN DIAMETER

PREPARATION: 20 MIN

COOKING: 8 MIN

For the cakes

  2 c flour

  1 tsp baking powder

  ½ tsp baking soda

  ⅓ c butter, softened

  2 eggs + 1 egg white

  1¾ c milk

  4 Tbsp pesto

  dash of pepper

For the filling

  5 oz tapenade olive spread

  3.5 oz cream cheese

  10 cherry tomatoes

Make the cakes. Preheat the oven to 350°. In a mixing bowl, combine the flour, baking powder, and baking soda. In another bowl, beat the one egg white until stiff peaks form, then add the two whole eggs and the butter and beat. Mix the contents of the two bowls together, then gradually add the milk, mixing well. Add the pesto and pepper and mix until all the ingredients are incorporated into the batter. Place the batter in small circles on a baking sheet. Bake for 8 minutes, then let cool.

Make the filling. Mix the tapenade and cream cheese together. Use a small spoon to spread this mixture on half of the cakes, then put the filled cakes and plain cakes together.

Decorate the whoopie pies by putting half a cherry tomato on top of each one; use a toothpick to attach them. You can eat these whoopie pies right away or keep them in the refrigerator up to 24 hours.

Idea: Try using black tapenade instead of green.

You can replace the feta in this recipe with fresh goat cheese. And for a real French flavor, try substituting a teaspoon of dried herbes de provence (found in the spice aisle) for the thyme.

Feta, thyme, and honey whoopie pies

MAKES 20 WHOOPIE PIES ABOUT
1 IN. IN DIAMETER

PREPARATION: 25 MIN

COOKING: 8 MIN

For the cakes

1⅔ c flour

1 tsp baking powder

1 tsp baking soda

dash of salt

¼ c butter, softened

1 whole egg + 1 egg white

For the filling

5 oz ricotta cheese

5 oz feta cheese

2 Tbsp honey

1 Tbsp fresh thyme, finely chopped

10 hazelnets or walnuts, chopped

dash of pepper

Make the cakes. Preheat the oven to 350°. In a mixing bowl, combine the flour, baking powder, baking soda, and salt. In another bowl, beat the butter and the whole egg. Add the dry ingredients to the butter and egg mixture and mix well. Beat the egg white until stiff peaks form, then add it to the batter and mix thoroughly. Place the batter in small circles on a baking sheet. Bake for 8 minutes, then let cool.

Make the filling. Mix the ricotta, feta, and honey. Add the thyme and nuts, then add pepper to taste. Mix everything well. Use a spoon to spread the filling on half of the whoopie pies, then assemble the pies. You can eat these whoopie pies right away or keep them in the refrigerator for up to 24 hours.

Variation: Try adding 1 tsp of curry powder to the cake batter.

You can sprinkle parmesan on your whoopie pies right before baking to add a little extra texture.

Parmesan whoopie pies with artichoke

MAKES 20 WHOOPIE PIES ABOUT
1 IN. IN DIAMETER

PREPARATION: 25 MIN

COOKING: 8 MIN

For the cakes

2 c flour

1 tsp baking powder

1 tsp baking soda

½ c grated parmesan

1 egg

½ c milk

3 Tbsp olive oil

For the filling

½ an onion

7 oz artichoke hearts, canned or frozen

the juice of 1 lemon

3 Tbsp olive oil

2 Tbsp pine nuts

salt and pepper to taste

Make the cakes. Preheat the oven to 350°. In a mixing bowl, combine the flour, baking powder, baking soda, and parmesan. In another bowl, beat the egg, milk, and olive oil, then add these ingredients to the dry ingredients and mix well. Place the batter in small circles on a baking sheet. Bake for 8 minutes, then let cool.

Make the filling. Finely mince the onion. Cut the artichoke hearts into small pieces, and put these, along with all the other ingredients for the filling, into a blender. Blend for 1 to 2 minutes.

Use a spoon to spread a bit of the cream on half of the cakes, then put the cakes together. You can eat these whoopie pies right away or keep them in the refrigerator for up to 24 hours.

Idea: Garnish the whoopie pies with a leaf of arugula and slice of radish; use a toothpick to attach them.

Sun-dried tomato and bacon whoopie pies

MAKES 20 WHOOPIE PIES ABOUT
¾ IN. IN DIAMETER

PREPARATION: 20 MIN

COOKING: 8 MIN

For the cakes

1⅔ c flour

1 tsp baking powder

½ tsp baking soda

⅓ c butter, softened

2 whole eggs + 1 egg white

1¾ c milk

2 Tbsp pine nuts

salt and pepper to taste

For the filling

¼ lb bacon, thinly sliced*

⅓ c sun-dried tomatoes in oil,
drained

*Note: For a real European flavor, make
these with speck (found at specialty
delis and meat counters) instead of
bacon.

Make the cakes. Preheat the oven to 350º. In a mixing bowl, combine the flour, baking powder, and baking soda. In another bowl, beat the whole eggs and the butter. Mix the wet and dry ingredients together, then gradually add the milk, mixing well. Beat the egg white until stiff peaks form, then add it to the batter. Add the pine nuts, salt, and pepper, and mix until all ingredients are incorporated. Place the batter in small circles on a baking sheet. Bake for 8 minutes, then let cool.

Prepare the filling. Fry the bacon then let it drain. Cut the meat into thin strips, then place a slice, along with a sun-dried tomato, between two cakes; use toothpicks to hold the whoopie pies together. Serve while still warm.

A variation on the traditional Russian blini, this smoked salmon whoopie pie is a gourmet appetizer. Try it also with smoked trout.

Buckwheat and smoked salmon whoopie pies

MAKES 30 WHOOPIE PIES ABOUT
¾ IN. IN DIAMETER

PREPARATION: 25 MIN

COOKING: 8 MIN

For the cakes

1 c flour

1 c buckwheat flour

1 tsp baking powder

1 tsp baking soda

1 large egg

¾ c milk

2 Tbsp dill, chopped

salt and pepper to taste

For the filling

½ lb smoked salmon

⅓ c cucumber (about ¼ of a medium cucumber)

5 Tbsp heavy whipping cream

2.5 oz fromage frais (or cream cheese)

½ tsp pink pepper

salt and pepper to taste

Make the cakes. Preheat the oven to 350°. In a mixing bowl, combine the two types of flour, baking powder, and baking soda. Add the egg and beat the mixture, then gradually add the milk. Mix well, then add half the dill and the salt and pepper. Mix until all the ingredients are mixed in. Place the batter in small circles on a baking sheet. Bake for 8 minutes, then let cool.

Make the filling. Chop 3 oz of the smoked salmon into very small pieces. Peel the cucumber, cut it in half, scoop out the seeds, then dice it into small pieces. In a mixing bowl, mix the cream and the fromage frais together. Add the chopped salmon, the cucumber, the remainder of the dill, and the pink pepper and mix well. Add salt and pepper to taste.

Use a small spoon to spread the filling on the flat sides of half of the cakes, then put the cakes together. Cut the rest of the smoked salmon into thin slices to garnish the tops of the whoopie pies. You can eat these whoopie pies right away or keep them in the refrigerator for up to 24 hours.

Tip: If you store these whoopie pies in the refrigerator, cover them with plastic wrap or put them in an airtight container so they don't dry out.

STACKPOLE BOOKS
5067 Ritter Road
Mechanicsburg, PA 17055
www.stackpolebooks.com

Printed in U.S.A.

10 9 8 7 6 5 4 3 2 1

First edition

ISBN 978-0-8117-1256-9

Cataloging-in-publication data is on file with the Library of Congress.

Editions Larousse
Publication: Isabelle Jeuge-Maynart and Ghislaine Stora
Managing editor: Delphine Blétry
Editing: Mathilde Piton, assisted by Johana Amsilli
Artistic direction: Emmanuel Chaspoul
Pagination: Miyo Edit

Stackpole Books
Translation: Kathryn Fulton
Cover design: Caroline M. Stover
Pagination: Tessa J. Sweigert

Corinne Jausserand warmly thanks: Ressource painters for their beautiful paints (www.ressource-peintures.com); Chiffonade for their lovely colored fabric (1 avenue de la Sablière 94370 Sucy-en-Brie); Himla for their table linens (www.himla.fr); and Kenwood for the loan of a food processor (www.kenwood.fr).

Thanks to Cathy, who always goes out of her way to find me pretty objects and beautiful fabrics. Thanks to everyone who helped and encouraged me in the making of this work. Thanks to Caroline, who I always enjoy working with and who tried all of these whoopie pies! And a little wink to Daniel and Valérie, who also got to try some whoopie pies—at least, when there were any left!